MR
Pri
Ser
Volu

The Quest for Literacy

Curriculum and Instructional Procedures for Teaching Reading and Writing to Students with Mental Retardation and Developmental Disabilities

by David S. Katims

A Publication of
The Division on Mental Retardation
and Developmental Disabilities of
The Council for Exceptional Children

Table of Contents

Forward

Literacy is a concept beyond simple demonstration of word recognition and rudimentary writing skills. Literacy is the act of reading to attain meaning from text and writing to communicate meaning. Helping students with mental retardation and other developmental disabilities achieve literacy has received little attention in professional literature in recent years. The Division on Mental Retardation and Developmental Disabilities of the Council for Exceptional Children is pleased to offer this <u>Prism Series</u> book to its members and others interested in teaching for literacy.

The author, Dr. David Katims, presents an optimistic and, to some, a provocative perspective on teaching reading and writing to students with mental retardation. In addition to clearly defining reading and offering suggestions for assessments, Dr. Katims provides numerous practical teaching tips and tools focused on helping students attain literacy. The Division is highly appreciative of David Katims' contribution the MRDD <u>Prism Series</u>.

Laurence Sargent
Colorado Springs

To Dr. Sue Allen Warren--Teacher, mentor, friend

vi

Preface

The Quest for Literacy: Curriculum and Instructional Procedures for Teaching Reading and Writing to Students with Mental Retardation addresses a topic that is underrepresented in the education of individuals with mental retardation. The concept and idea of merging literacy with students who have mental retardation has not yet reached acceptance in our society — even among many advocates for people with disabilities.

Literacy pessimism toward individuals with mental retardation is rooted in the conviction that these students are incapable of anything greater than a functional existence—thus, the preeminence of functional approaches in our schools. Even professional organizations that position themselves as leaders in the field of mental retardation and disability fail to substantively address literacy in their publications.

This monograph offers a different viewpoint towards literacy education for students with mild to moderate mental retardation. It presents a collection of methods, materials, and techniques for assessing and teaching students to become successfully literate. It is not intended to be an encyclopedic or comprehensive description of all techniques appropriate for teaching reading and writing. The purpose is to inform special and general educators, related services personnel, administrators, and perhaps even policy makers about contemporary approaches to educating students with mental retardation.

The information is presented from the belief that reading and writing are integrated, constructivist activities that should be taught from the earliest years of a student's school experience. Literacy themes addressed in this monograph include: A Foundation of Literacy Instruction, Literacy

Assessment for Students with Mental Retardation, Teaching Word Identification and Comprehension Strategies, Teaching Writing Strategies, and finally, the last section, written by Dr. Laurence Sargent and Suzanne Doyle, highlights practices utilized within classrooms by effective special educators.

This monograph is dedicated to Dr. Sue Allen Warren, whom I first met at Boston University in the early 1980's. Dr. Warren came to exert the greatest influence on me, both personally and professionally, of anyone I have ever encountered. I was fortunate enough to have her serve as my dissertation chair, and guide me through the process of my first research endeavor. Sue Allen Warren was Professor of special education at Boston University, a clinical psychologist, a humanitarian, an advocate and an educator. She was a member of the Classification and Terminology Committee of AAMR under the Chairmanship of Herbert Grossman, M.D. She was also past President of AAMR and the American Psychological Association's Division on Mental Retardation. Professor Warren guided and influenced me in so many ways that words cannot do her justice. I simply wish to acknowledge her, and her admonition to . . . "Do the right thing". Unfortunately, Dr. Warren passed away in November of 1997—her family, students, colleagues and friends remember her and miss her.

I would also like to acknowledge Joni Chavez-Martell, M. A., for her assistance with this monograph. Joni joined me as my Graduate Research Assistant at the time when I took on the task of beginning this project. Her intelligence and insight were enormously important to me throughout the process. In so many ways Joni reminds me of Sue Allen Warren—particularly her unbridled optimism for the human race.

David S. Katims
The University of Texas at San Antonio
San Antonio, Texas
December 1999

Part One:

A Foundation for Literacy Instruction

Can Students with Mental Retardation Learn to Read and Write?

The reality that students identified with mental retardation can learn to read and write has been documented in research literature for some time (for example see, Cegelka & Cegelka, 1970; Dunn, 1956; Conners, 1992; Orlando, 1973; Singh & Singh, 1986; Stanovich, 1985). More than two hundred years ago, Jean Marc-Gaspard Itard, the "father" of special education, taught a young boy with mental retardation to recognize letters, arrange them in words, form sentences, and write. Seguin advanced the work of his mentor, Itard, by directing students with mental retardation to first draw lines and angles, write letters of the alphabet, match wooden letters to alphabet cards, and eventually read words and sentences. Seguin became the greatest European influence on the development of educational programs for people with mental retardation in this country (Seguin, 1860).

Throughout the next two centuries, innovative teachers and researchers used a variety of methods, materials, techniques and technologies to teach people with mental retardation to become literate. History records one teacher who awoke his students each morning at dawn with the ringing of a Chinese gong, and then used phosphorus pencils in a darkened room to get them to attend to letters, words and sentences. Other inventive teachers used finger tracing, wooden letters, film projectors, language experience approaches, computer-assisted instruction, immersion approaches, flash cards, sentence strips, basal readers with highly controlled vocabulary, and even a multicolor alphabet approach. All of these early pioneers were successful due to their students making progress toward becoming literate (see Katims (2000), for a history of literacy instruction).

Today, over 600,000 school age students (ages 6-21 years old) with mental retardation are served in our public schools (U. S. Department of Education). Perhaps as many as 90 percent of these students fall within the mild to high functioning moderate range of disability. Unfortunately, current classroom instructional programs tend to focus primarily on teaching social, vocational, and daily living skills to the exclusion of literacy instruction beyond a basic functional level. Many survey textbooks in special education and mental retardation perpetuate "literacy pessimism" among professionals because they do not address or emphasize the importance of teaching reading and writing to this population. The authors of these textbooks focus on identification and causation issues, without substantively addressing the literacy characteristics of students with mental retardation, techniques for assessing their literacy abilities, or methodologies for teaching them to become literate.

There are also well known national organizations for special education professionals that seem to perpetuate this lack of literacy optimism through minimizing literacy and its importance for people with mental retardation. Although learning how to read and write printed language appears to dominate the early schooling of most children around the world, when it comes to the literacy education for students identified with mental retardation, limited optimism is readily apparent.

Is There More Than One Way to Teach Literacy?

In the United States, literacy education for students with mental retardation has at best been minimized in our schools. Without exception, every review of the literature on reading and writing for individuals with mental retardation indicates they perform well below their own mental age. This denotes that the literacy potential for many of these students remains largely untapped. Since there has historically been a de-emphasis on real literacy instruction for students with mild to moderate mental retardation in this country, a growing number of special education professionals question common classroom practices.

Currently, two literacy orientations are predominantly used by teachers of students with mental retardation that can be characterized as either *functional* or *traditional* approaches. The *functional approach*, most often utilized in special education classrooms, is concerned with teaching rudimentary functional, or survival skills that transfer directly to the student's home, community, and work environments. Teachers may spend years instructing students to use a telephone book, print their name, or recognize community words such as "Poison", "Men' "Women" "Exit" or "Do Not Enter". By assuming a functional curriculum approach for these students, practitioners de-emphasize real literacy learning, and instead concentrate their curricula heavily on social, personal, and vocationally related skills. Unfortunately, what may be functional for one student may not be so for another student. Teachers who employ this approach often spend much time teaching functional skills to students for whom it may be inappropriate. Also, unless functional skills are taught within real life contexts (such as in community-based instruction), generalization of functional skills is questionable.

The other orientation to literacy education for students with mental retardation is the *traditional approach*. Traditional teachers also focus their curriculum on social, personal, and vocational skills, but approach literacy instruction from a point of view which stresses repetitive, isolated drill and practice of decontextualized, small bits of information—information that is presented out of the context of connected words in sentences or books. This approach attempts to teach isolated mastery of a linear set of subskills, which rarely engage students in reading well constructed, connected texts containing multiple sentences.

Since people with disabilities have great difficulty mastering these isolated subskills, they do not gain access to participation in the higher processes of using literacy as a tool for communication, obtaining information, or reading for pleasure. This approach is deeply rooted in the behavioral perspective to human learning in that advocates believe a task analysis must be performed on skills to be taught (reading or writing in this case), and principles of reinforcement applied to shape the behavior to the desired level (Katims, 1994).

A contemporary and newly emerging approach to literacy instruction advocated by an increasing number of professionals, is the use of **progressive** instructional methods. Teachers who use a progressive instructional orientation have demonstrated that students with mental retardation have the potential and ability to become increasingly literate. Progressive instruction supports an integrated and constructivist approach to literacy instruction in which skills are taught within the context of connected sentences and paragraphs. Students are given the opportunity to interact with written language in many forms that enable them to construct meaning from real texts. For example, classroom practices that place words within the larger language contexts of sentence strips, flipcharts, texts containing multiple sentences, and books, assist students to further their literacy skills and strategies. Students improve their literacy skills through actually reading and writing real text. This is something foreign to the education of students with mental retardation. Conners (1992), for example, notes that in the general education classroom, the focus of reading instruction has moved toward students **constructing**, or gaining **meaning** from print—not so in the education of students with mental retardation, which tends to focus on decoding skills in isolation.

Figure 1.1 illustrates the **traditional**, decontextualized, or as some might say, bottom-up approach to literacy instruction in contrast to the **progressive**, contextualized, or top-down approach to literacy instruction. The traditional approach begins instruction with students identifying letters of the alphabet. They progress to assembling letters of the alphabet to devise words, and then use these words to read sentences. This is a *readiness* approach to literacy education where the subskills thought to underlie reading (letter-name knowledge, discrimination and association, and visual, auditory, and perceptual abilities) are assumed to be skills that must be taught to prepare the student for the challenges of formal reading instruction. In other words, background knowledge, the meaning of print, creating their own written products, or learning about the forms and functions of print may not be emphasized until lower level skills are mastered.

Progressive instruction emphasizes from the very beginning that students must use background knowledge and strategies to negotiate with text in meaningful ways to gain comprehension of what is written. Students are taught to construct meaning from books read out loud to them, and then ultimately able to read alone.

Another aspect to progressive instruction is the acknowledgement of an *emergent literacy orientation* (Katims, 1991). Those ascribing to an emergent literacy orientation view the reading and writing behaviors of young children (scribbling and/or picture reading) as important parts of literacy development that may extend well into the upper grades for students with mental retardation. Emergent literacy techniques involve the powerful idea that literacy development begins well before young children actually begin to read and write conventionally. Reading and writing are best learned from active engagement in everyday, meaningful communication activities, to help children understand the forms and functions of written language. Literacy is no longer regarded as simply a cognitive skill, but as a complex activity with social, linguistic, and psychological aspects. Evidence portrays that with intensive daily instruction over a long period of time,

Figure 1.1
Comparison of Traditional and Progressive Approaches to
Teaching Literacy

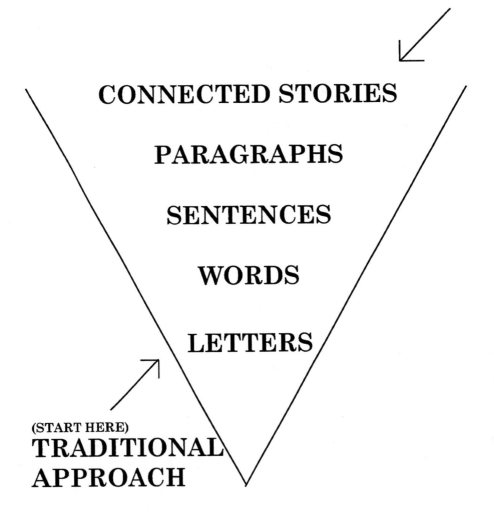

**PROGRESSIVE
APPROACH**

(START HERE)

CONNECTED STORIES

PARAGRAPHS

SENTENCES

WORDS

LETTERS

(START HERE)
**TRADITIONAL
APPROACH**

students with mild to moderate mental retardation can make measurable gains in the use of word identification and reading comprehension strategies, writing strategies, and understanding how written language works.

The first documented account of an emergent approach to literacy with a developmentally delayed child, who had physical, sensory, cognitive, and health disabilities, was published in 1975. In a book titled, Cushla and her books, a grandmother chronicles her granddaughter's growth in literacy (Butler, 1975). She describes immersion into a world rich and full of oral language experiences, storybook readings, and the extraordinary support of her immediate and extended family.

Cushla's mother, born and raised in a family of book lovers, started reading to Cushla at the age of four months to fill the long hours when Cushla would cry inconsolably. As the years passed, Cushla demonstrated a wide variety of vocal, verbal, physical, cognitive, and emotional responses to literature in her home. She was able to follow a story line, understand story actions, and identify with main characters within stories. She asked questions about, and interacted with books in many ways, including memorizing entire books verbatim. Eventually Cushla was able to demonstrate independent reenactments with her favorite books.

What Statements Might Typify A Teacher With A Progressive Literacy Perspective?

Special education professionals who believe in, and support a progressive literacy approach to instruction may be represented by the following distinctive views:
- Students identified with mental retardation can become literate. For example, a ten year old student with mild mental retardation in elementary school may not read like other ten year olds, yet he can demonstrate significant progress in reading and writing, and continue

to grow in literacy with intensive and extensive instruction.

- Measured intelligence quotient (IQ) is not the sole indicator of ultimate literacy achievement for students with mental retardation. Early and continued exposure to literacy, and good instruction are significant factors for these students.
- Progressive literacy teachers know the importance of the reading and writing behaviors of young children that precede and develop into conventional literacy (such as scribbling or drawing a letter to grandma, or pretending to read a book).
- Progressive literacy teachers believe that students master literacy skills as a result of authentic reading and writing.
- Reading aloud to children may be the single most important literacy activities teachers can provide to their students.
- A child's initial encounters with print should focus on meaning, not on exact word recognition.
- Reading and writing are complimentary to one another and should be taught simultaneously. Reading promotes and supports writing, while writing promotes and supports reading.
- There are three basic strands of beginning reading behavior, which develop separately but concurrently: (a) attention to the functions of print (why people write); (b) attention to the forms of print (commercial logos, pictures, print, cursive); and (c) attention to the conventions of print (left to write, from the top of a page to the bottom, use of punctuation, etc.).
- Processes that enable children to acquire reading ability include: (a) observations of people engaged in literacy (a teacher reading to her students); (b) collaboration with others in performing literate acts (making a get-well card for a sick friend); and (c) practice with literacy materials (looking at books and using writing materials).

- Writing development for the beginning writer may be characterized by children moving from (a) playfully making marks on paper; (b) through communicating messages on paper; (c) to making conventional texts such as notes or stories.
- As students begin to become more conventionally literate, they must be taught that reading is an active search for meaning; the purpose of reading is to construct meaning from text.
- Reading is a strategic process in which a child must think about ways to construct meaning from text.
- Reading, writing, listening, and speaking are all parts of the comprehension process.
- Students can be taught to "self-talk" as they begin to apply learning strategies to decode unknown words and enhance their reading comprehension.
- Reading is an interactive process whereby the reader attempts to understand what the writer has put down on print.

Is There Recent Evidence of Literacy Achievement For Students With Mental Retardation?

One of the most recent investigations providing evidence of literacy achievement involves an exploratory assessment of 132 students with mild to moderate mental retardation (Katims, 1999). In this study, students' IQs ranged from 76 to 29 with an average IQ of 55. Of the 132 students assessed, 54 students (41%) demonstrated an instructional level in word recognition, and 34 students (26%) demonstrated an instructional level in narrative reading comprehension on an Analytical Reading Inventory (ARI). This is an exciting discovery as it confirms that a notable portion of this population can read.

Table 1.1 illustrates the results of the study investigating the word recognition and reading comprehension of elementary and secondary students with mental retardation.

Table 1.1
Results of Reading Assessment on an Analytical Reading Inventory by students (percent and number of students out of 132) with Mild to Moderate Mental Retardation

Reading Level	Percent and Number of Students for Each Reading Level In Word Recognition	Percent and Number of Students For Each Reading Level In Reading Comprehension
Primer	22.6 (10)	31.9 (14)
1	33.9 (15)	17.7 (8)
2	22.8 (10)	6.9 (3)
3	4.7 (2)	7.3 (3)
4	18.1 (8)	7.3 (3)
5	9.4 (4)	7.3 (3)
6	12.5 (5)	0
Cumulative Total	41.33% (54)	26.1% (34)

Overall, 54 out of 132 students (41%) were able to achieve an instructional level in word recognition at least at a primer level. The remaining 78 students did not score high enough to be measured by the ARI. In the area of reading comprehension, 34 students out of 132 students (26%) were able to achieve an instructional level at least at the primer level. The remaining 98 students did not score high enough to be measured by the ARI.

The reading level achieved most often by students in word recognition was grade 1 at which 15 students (34%) scored. The reading level achieved most often by students in reading comprehension was Primer at which 14 students (32%) in the group scored.

In a comparison of word recognition and reading comprehension achievement, 63% of the students (34 out of 54) who achieved an instructional level in word recognition were able to achieve an instructional level in narrative reading comprehension. This confirms other studies of the reading achievement for this population in which word recognition tends to be stronger than reading comprehension (see Crawley & Parmar, 1995).

Of those students who achieved at least a Primer level on the ARI, their oral reading could be described as word-by-word, choppy, halting, and in need of much aid by the examiner for unknown words. Their oral reading contained numerous repetitions, omissions, and insertions. Students' syntactic and semantic miscues tended to be the most common type of errors in their oral reading. For example, students demonstrated great difficulty in using context clues to decode unknown words. They tended to guess randomly at the pronunciation of unknown words relying primarily on the initial sounds in words, without regard to meaning, or sense of the sentence.

On a separate dictation task in which writing was assessed, teachers read two sentences while students were directed to write them as correctly. Students demonstrated the ability to hear phonemes (sounds) in dictated words and write the correct grapheme (letter or letter combinations). Students progressed from grade level to grade level in their ability to hear phonemes and correctly write graphemes from two sentences dictated by an examiner. Out of a possible score of 37 separate phonemes, elementary students were able write an average of 9, middle school students 22, and high school students 26. In a final task, students were asked to write as many words as they could in ten minutes. They performed similarly as above in that the average number of words written by students increased from elementary (9.5), to middle school (11.1), to high school (11.9).

These findings indicate that many of the students who participated in this study demonstrated the ability to recognize words, comprehend narrative reading passages, and write words and sentences correctly. The students also showed a clear developmental progression in literacy competence from elementary, to middle school, to high school on each of the literacy tasks.

Although a statistically significant difference existed between the IQs of the 54 students who achieved an instructional level on the ARI (average IQ = 61), and the remaining 78 students (average IQ = 49), the results indicated neither grade level (elementary, middle school, or high school), or IQ scores predicted students' performance on word recognition or comprehension.

It seems as though IQ was important to differentiate "readers" from "non-readers" within the 132 students assessed. Group I, the lower IQ group, did not achieve an instructional level on the ARI ("non-readers"), while Group II, the higher IQ group, achieved an instructional level at least at the primer reading level on the ARI in either word recognition and/or reading comprehension ("readers"). However, for Group II ("readers") students, IQ was not the sole determinant of their success as readers. In other words, many students with lower measured IQs either equaled or performed at higher grade levels than students with higher measured IQs in Group II. Since the 54 students in Group II represented both high and low socioeconomic status backgrounds, as well as a cross-section of ethnicity and race in the school district, it is believed that higher performing Group II readers with relatively lower IQs were possibly exposed to early and intensive literacy interventions.

One final distinction was made for Group II Readers. Seventeen students (31%) and 6 students (18%), respectively, achieved a fourth grade or higher level in word recognition, and narrative comprehension. Researchers differentiate between learning to read—learning to recognize and sound out words and to read fairly simple materials with ease and fluency—to reading to learn—becoming able to use reading as a tool for learning new things. The stage of reading to learn is crucial to academic success and typically begins at about the fourth grade. Unfortunately, this is also the period in which most students with mild mental retardation tend to bog down in their reading ability due to the difficulty of more demanding texts.

Part Two

Literacy Assessment for Students with Mental Retardation

Why Assess?

Assessment is a valuable process that enables professionals to select appropriate instructional procedures for students. It is the foundation of special education as it allows teachers to individualize instruction. One purpose of informal assessment in the classroom is to determine for whom prereferral intervention is needed. As the name suggests, prereferral intervention teams consult with, assist, and support classroom educators in developing adaptive instructional systems or remedial techniques for struggling students.

Another purpose of assessment is to make a decision about classification. During the formal testing process, the multidisciplinary team asks questions such as: "Does Marisa demonstrate the characteristics of someone with a learning disability?" If so, "Does she seem to have a verbal or a non-verbal learning disability?" Or, "Does Josue present data that might lead us to believe he could qualify for services under the category of mental retardation?" If so, "What level of mental retardation does he seem to have based on measured intellectual performance and adaptive behavior evaluation?" At the time of classification, the multidisciplinary team usually makes an informed placement decision using the available assessment data from multiple sources.

A third purpose of assessment is to develop the individualized education plan (IEP) for instructional purposes. The Individuals with Disabilities Education Act (IDEA, P.L. 105-17) as amended in 1997 requires multiple components be addressed in the development of each student's IEP, and includes the following:

- Documentation of the student's Present Level of Performance (PLOP).
- Statements of specific Annual Goals for each student.
- Specifying Short-Term Instructional Objectives whereby annual goals will be attained.

Teachers using progressive instructional techniques strive to create a balanced curriculum for individual students. The balance is achieved when teachers combine the IEP objectives of teaching age and stage appropriate social skills (interactions with others); personal skills (dressing, grooming, if necessary); and vocational skills with literacy education.

What Stages of Literacy Development Are Important For Classroom Assessment?

A starting point for special educators is to understand that children (with and without disabilities) progressively move forward, in stage-like fashion, as they develop from preconventional readers and writers, toward competency as conventional readers and writers. By understanding these developmental stages and levels of literacy, teachers can identify each student's present level of performance and plan instruction accordingly.

- **Preconventional Readers and Writers**
  Students display curiosity about books and tools that are used for reading and writing. They enjoy listening to stories read aloud, and have favorites they request. They also enjoy holding the book and turning pages. Participating in nursery rhymes and Sesame Street songs are favorite activities. These children may be able to recognize the first letter of their name and many can draw stick-figure pictures in an attempt to communicate and convey telling a story in "writing". Thus, exposure to good quality children's literature, and literacy-rich experiences, are of the utmost importance during this initial developmental stage.

• **Emergent Readers and Writers**

Students are curious about reading and writing and "see" themselves as potentially literate. They rely on pictures to tell the story, but are beginning to focus on print in books. They easily recognize environmental print (such as logos representing their favorite restaurant and soft drink). They are developing a print to speak match—understanding that print has meaning. During read aloud, they may chime in with a familiar or predictable word or phrase. Also, after hearing a rhyming or predictable book, they may often engage in pretend readings. These independent reenactments, or emergent storybook readings, are at the root of literacy development for the young child. They involve the child "retelling" favorite stories to themselves, their friends, stuffed animals, or pets, and facilitate the child's developing conventions of literacy. Children may also scribble a letter to grandma, a get-well note to a sick friend, help mother create a shopping list, or make a holiday wish list. At this stage, children can write letters of the alphabet and use invented spellings in which phonetic relationships can be seen (btr for better). Daily exposure to literacy and print continues to be important.

• **Early Readers and Writers**

Students see themselves as readers and writers of simple word patterns such as consonant-vowel-consonant rhyming words. They know most letter sounds and recognize simple words such as it, dog, cat, and, the, and so on. They can read simple books independently and understand what they are reading. With prompting and encouragement, students may be able to retell the important parts of a story after having it read aloud, or reading it aloud to themselves. They can also print their name (may have letter reversals and disproportionate letter sizes).

• **Developing Readers and Writers**

Students are now able to read with fairly good

competence. They can read words they have never encountered using a number of strategies such as the use of sentence structure, meaning, and phonetic clues. These students are refining their self-monitoring and self-checking strategies. They know many words by sight and are able to retell the beginning, middle, and end of stories with great accuracy. Students can write short, simple sentences, with both conventional and invented spellings.

- **Fluent Readers and Writers**

Students are completely confident and comfortable readers and writers. These students are at the stage where they can read to learn, as opposed to learning to read in the previous stages. Students use many strategies to read both narrative and expository texts in the areas of social studies and science. They can write complete sentences to create a story and engage in the writing process in which subsequent drafts of papers are rewritten until a final paper is prepared.

Where to Begin?

An appropriate place to initiate integration of literacy into the curriculum is by obtaining a clear understanding of individual student's strengths and difficulties in reading and writing. This is best done by analyzing questions such as: "What does Tommy believe about reading and writing?" "What strategies does Jesse use to identify unknown words?" "How well does Carlos write a descriptive paragraph on skateboarding?" "At which stage does William fit in the scheme of conventional reading progression (preconventional, emergent, early)?"

The following concepts assist teachers with identifying strengths and difficulties, as well as for planning, assessing, and instructing students. These terms accompany the template shown in Figure 2.1, and may be used to record student's strengths (+) and difficulties (-) in these areas:

- *Concepts About Print* refers to the student's knowledge of what reading and writing mean. It includes understanding the conventions of the English language such as where to start reading on a page, what a period means, the difference between pictures and words, and so on.

- *Word Recognition* involves the cueing, or identification system a student uses to determine how to pronounce a word. There are a number of word recognition strategies:

  -*Sight words* are "see-say words" a student can recognize on sight.

  -*Phonetic analysis* involves the student using the sound-symbol relationship within words to sound them out (for example, the word mat has three phonemes (/m/ /a/ /t/).

  -*Syntactic analysis* means the student uses knowledge of the sense of the language to decode an unknown word. For example, knowing that a noun is the only possible answer in the following sentence. "John went to the store to get a _____".

  -*Semantic analysis* means understanding that the words in sentences must make sense. When discerning an unknown word, a student who understands semantics will not make wild guesses about the pronunciation of a word; he or she will consider "what makes sense". The combination of syntactic analysis and semantic analysis is commonly called using context clues.

- *Comprehension/Retelling* Competence involves the student demonstrating understanding of a story by correctly answering a set of questions about a passage. Students may also be asked to "retell" everything they remember about the story as another measure of comprehension.

- *Reading Fluency* means the smoothness and expression a student reads with. Questions that can be asked include: "Is the student's reading stilted, halting, and bogged down with word identification, or is the reading smooth, clear, and full of expression?".

- *Writing Competence* means the student's ability to write upper and lower case letters, words, sentences, and paragraphs using spelling, punctuation, meaning, and syntax.
- *Attitude Toward Literacy* involves the student's response to various types and levels of reading and writing. For example, does the student understand the purpose of reading is to determine what the author of the text is saying, not just to decode each word in a passage, one-by-one? Does the student seem to be anxious, frustrated, or calm and confident in his or her reading/writing?

Figure 2.1
A Template for Viewing Literacy

Student'sName _____Date _____

- **Estimated Stage of Literacy (check most appropriate):**

Preconventional __ Emergent __ Early __ Developing __ Fluent ___

Concepts About   Word Recognition
       Print
+   -   +   -

Comprehension/Retelling   Reading Fluency
       Competence
+   -   +   -

Writing Competence   Attitude Toward Literacy
+   -   +   -

What Are Some Assessment Techniques and Devices?

Presented on page 25 are brief descriptions of several assessment tools used successfully by special education teachers in determining individual student's strengths and difficulties in reading and writing. Of course it is not necessary to use all these assessment devices for each student. Teachers wanting to obtain these devices, can contact the publisher directly for ordering information, or contact a commercial or university bookstore.

- **Informal Structured Literacy Observation Checklists**
  A great deal of information concerning student's understanding of printed language can be gained through the use of observation checklists. A slight modification of a checklist developed by Morrow (1993) is presented in Figure 2.2.

Figure 2.2

A Checklist for Assessing Early Literacy Development

Name_____Date _____

**Attitudes Toward Reading and
Voluntary Reading Behavior**

	ALWAYS	SOMETIMES	NEVER
Voluntarily looks at or reads books	____	____	____
Asks to be read to	____	____	____
Listens attentively while being read to	____	____	____
Responds with questions and comments to stories read to him or her	____	____	____

Concepts about Books	ALWAYS	SOMETIMES	NEVER
Knows that a book is for reading	____	____	____
Can identify the front, back, top, and bottom of a book	____	____	____
Can turn pages properly	____	____	____
Knows the difference between the print and the pictures	____	____	____
Knows that pictures on a page are related to what the print says	____	____	____
Knows where to begin reading	____	____	____
Knows what a title is	____	____	____
Knows what an author is	____	____	____

Knows what an illustrator is _____   _____   _____

Comprehension of Text ALWAYS   SOMETIMES   NEVER

	ALWAYS	SOMETIMES	NEVER
Attempts to read storybooks resulting in well-formed stories	_____	_____	_____
Retells stories	_____	_____	_____
Includes story structure elements in story retellings:			
Setting	_____	_____	_____
Theme	_____	_____	_____
Sequences	_____	_____	_____
Resolution	_____	_____	_____
Responds to text after reading or listening with comments or Questions	_____	_____	_____

Concepts about Print	ALWAYS	SOMETIMES	NEVER
Knows print is read from left to right	_____	_____	_____
Knows that oral language can be written down and then read	_____	_____	_____
Knows what a letter is and can point one out on a page	_____	_____	_____
Knows what a word is and can point one out on a printed page	_____	_____	_____
Reads environmental print	_____	_____	_____
Reads Logos (McDonalds, etc)	_____	_____	_____
Recognizes some words by sight	_____	_____	_____
Can name rhyming words	_____	_____	_____

Can identify and name upper-
and lowercase letters of
the alphabet　　　　_____　　_____　　　_____

Associates consonants and
their initial and final
sounds (including hard and
soft c and g)　　　　_____　　_____　　　_____

Associates vowels with
their corresponding long
and short sounds (a-acorn,
apple; e-eagle, egg; i-ice,
igloo; o-oats, octopus; u-
unicorn, umbrella)　　　_____　　_____　　　_____

Knows the consonant
digraph sounds (ch, ph,
Sh, th, wh)　　　　_____　　_____　　　_____

Can blend and segment
phonemes in words　　_____　　_____　　　_____

Uses context, syntax, and
semantics to identify words　_____　　_____　　_____

Can count syllables in words　_____　　_____　　_____

Attempts reading by attending
to picture clues and print　_____　　_____　　　_____

Guesses and predicts words
based on knowledge of
sound-symbol correspondence _____　　_____　　　_____

Writing Development　　ALWAYS　SOMETIMES　NEVER

Explores with writing
materials　　　　　_____　　_____　　　_____

Dictates stories, sentences
or words he or she wants
written down　　　　_____　　_____　　　_____

Copies letters and words　_____　　_____　　　_____

Independently attempts
writing to convey
meaning, regardless of
writing level   _____   _____   _____

Can write his or her name   _____   _____   _____

Collaborates with others in
writing experience   _____   _____   _____

Writes for functional
purposes   _____   _____   _____

Check ( ) the level or levels at which
the child is writing

_____ uses drawing for writing

_____ differentiates between writing
and drawing

_____ uses scribble writing for writing

_____ uses letter-like forms for writing

_____ uses learned letters in random
fashion for writing

_____ uses invented spelling for writing

_____ writes conventionally with
conventional spelling

Mechanics for Writing	ALWAYS	SOMETIMES	NEVER
Forms uppercase letters legibly	_____	_____	_____
Forms lowercase letters legibly	_____	_____	_____
Writes from left to right	_____	_____	_____
Leaves spaces between words	_____	_____	_____
Uses capital letters when necessary	_____	_____	_____
Uses periods in appropriate places	_____	_____	_____
Uses commas in appropriate places	_____	_____	_____

- **Observation Survey of Early Literacy Achievement**

Clay, M. M. (1993). An observation survey of early literacy achievement. Heinemann: Portsmouth, NH.

Clay developed a structured observation device to obtain both a quantitative and qualitative measure of individual children's knowledge of early reading and writing. According to the author, the Observation Survey provides a valid and reliable measure of the student's ability to perform a number of tasks related to early literacy achievement. The Early Literacy Observation includes:

Running Record: The student reads several passages while the teacher marks all words read correctly, and notes miscues and unknown words. The objective of a running record is to determine the processes by which the student monitors and corrects their own reading performance.

Letter Identification: Students are asked to identify 54 upper and lower case letters of the alphabet. Credit is given for each letter correctly named, or by saying the sound (phoneme) of letters.

Concepts About Print: This is used to determine student's awareness of the conventions of print and books. The 24- item test includes such concepts as directionality (left to write, up to down), the role of print (not the pictures) in telling the story, the concepts of "letters" and "words", punctuation, and so forth. The test can be used with nonreaders because the child is asked to identify certain features as the story is read aloud by the examiner.

Word Test: The student is asked to read word lists that contain 20 words each. The objective of this assessment is to determine the students strengths and difficulties with specific consonants (b,d,p), consonant blends (bl, cl, sw), clusters (spl), long vowels ("a" as in ape), short vowels ("e" as in elephant), vowel digraphs (ou, ea), and so on.

Writing Vocabulary: This task allows examination of the quality and quantity of each student's writing behavior. Students are given several blank sheets of paper and directed to write as many words as possible in 10 minutes. If the student appears confused, the examiner prompts with suggestions such as: "Can you write your name?" "Do you know how to write 'I' or 'a' or 'is' or 'to'?" "Do you know how to write things you like to do?, and so on.

Hearing Sounds in Words (dictation): Each student is asked to write two sentences that are dictated by the examiner. A count is then conducted to record the student's representation of sounds they hear (phonemes) by the number of corresponding letters or letter combinations (graphemes) they write.

- **Test of Early Reading Ability-2**

   Reid, D. K., Hresko, W. P., & Hammill, D. D. (1991). *Test of early reading ability (2nd ed.).* Austin, TX: Pro-Ed, Inc.

   This is an individually administered, 46-item structured measure of student's ability to attribute meaning to printed symbols, knowledge of the alphabet and its function, and understanding of the conventions of print. Students are asked to respond to: (a) items designed to measure their ability to construct meaning from print, including awareness of print in environmental context, knowledge of relations among vocabulary items, and awareness of print in disconnected discourse; (b) knowledge of the alphabet and its function, including letter naming and alphabet recitation, and oral reading; (c) conventions of written language, including book handling, responding to other print conventions, and proof reading. Teachers can use the national norms that come with the test, or use it as a criterion referenced test to measure progress in literacy-orientation curriculums.

- **Test of Early Written Language-2**

   Hresko, W. P., Herron, S. R., & Peak, P. K. (1996). Test of early written language (2nd ed.). Austin, TX: Pro-Ed, Inc.

   This individually administered early writing assessment

is composed of two subtests. The Basic Writing component measures the mechanical aspects of writing and includes: students drawing pictures of their favorite television character, and telling about the picture, pointing to different writing utensils, showing the direction of writing across the page, and writing their own name. Subsequent items on the subtest, require the students to construct sentences from words randomly strung together.

The second subtest, titled Contextual Writing, measures the student's ability to produce a writing sample. Students are shown a picture and then asked to write a story. Two versions are presented. For younger students, a simple scenario is provided that shows three pictures depicting a sequential scene. For older students, a complex scene is provided. The combination of the two subtests yields a Global Writing Quotient that allows for a more complete understanding of the student's writing abilities. Norms are provided to compare student's performance with a national sample. The tests can be used to determine strengths and difficulties for individual students in the area of early written language.

- **The Analytical Reading Inventory**
  Woods, M. L. , & Moe, A. J. (1999). *Analytical reading inventory (6th edition)*. Merrill: Upper Saddle River, New Jersey.

The ARI is an individually administered informal classroom reading inventory, used to observe, analyze, and record data about student's reading strategies. It is composed of a series of graded passages that reflect the type of texts assigned in school (narrative and expository passages). The ARI measures student's general level of word recognition, that includes their strengths and difficulties in oral reading, narrative text comprehension, expository text reading, and listening capacity (the ability to comprehend stories read aloud). Teachers are able to obtain three reading levels: Independent (the level at which the students reads well independently), instructional (the level at which reading instruction should be based), and frustrational (the level of reading a student should never have to read). A qualitative analysis of student's attitudes towards different reading levels is also obtained.

- **Cloze Reading Inventory**

De Santi, R. J., Casbergue, R. M., & Sullivan, V. G. (1986). *Cloze reading inventory.* Boston, MA: Allyn & Bacon, Inc.

The purposes of the Cloze Reading Inventory are to identify individual student's reading abilities, attendant strengths and difficulties, and the appropriate levels of instructional material. The inventory allows the teacher to measure reading achievement, determine independent, instructional, and frustrational reading levels, and diagnose reading strengths and difficulties. The inventory measures reading comprehension through the use of Cloze passages. These are passages with blanks; where deletions are made, the reader is expected to insert (write) a word in each blank. Word recognition and word identification are measured through the use of word lists. An example of a Cloze sentence is, "The rabbit ate the lettuce". Reconstruction to the Cloze format, the same sentence reads, "The _____ ate the lettuce."

- **Reading Miscue Inventory: Alternative Procedures**

Goodman, Y. M., Watson, D. J. & Burke, C. L. (1987). *Reading miscue inventory: Alternative procedures.* New York: Richard C. Owen Publishers, Inc.

The Reading Miscue Inventory (RMI) allows teachers to gain insight into individual student's reading processes, as well as provide a qualitative analysis of student's oral reading skills. The RMI evaluates why miscues (word errors, or faults) occur and assumes they are derived from the language and thoughts that readers use to construct meaning from reading. The miscues are analyzed to assist in the interpretation of the student's reading processes. For example, for each miscue made during oral reading, the teacher determines the following information:

- *Syntactic Acceptability* is concerned with the degree to which the reader produces acceptable grammatical structures (for example, subject-verb agreement).
- *Semantic Acceptability* focuses on the success with which the reader produces meaning from the text (for example, "he took the basket and went to the well for some water, instead of. . . he took a bucket and went. .). The dialect of the reader is always taken into consideration when considering syntactic and semantic acceptability of miscues.
- *Change the Meaning* is concerned with whether semantically and syntactically acceptable miscues *Change the Meaning* of the author's intentions.
- *Self Correction* is concerned with whether the student attempts to Self Correct their miscues.
- *Graphic Similarity* refers to a miscue that looks like the text being read (then for than, heard for had, or away for any).
- *Sound Similarity* refers to a miscue that sounds like the text being read (funny for phony, well for we'll, or bump for pump).

Since construction of meaning of the text is the focus in a Reading Miscue Inventory, each student is asked to relate an oral or written retelling of the story.

- **Brigance Diagnostic Comprehensive Inventory of Basic Skills**
  Brigance, A. H. (1983). *Brigance diagnostic comprehensive inventory of basic skills.* North Billerica, MA: Curriculum Associates.
  The Brigance Test is an individually administered

criterion-referenced instrument. Criterion-Referenced tests target student's performance on tasks that relate to specific instructional objectives. This test is designed to analyze strengths and difficulties in specific skill areas, and as a basis for instructional planning. The CIBS yields information that can be used to develop a curriculum for individual students. The following relevant areas can be assessed by the CIBS:

Word Recognition Grade Placement	*Word Analysis*
Oral Reading	*Spelling*
Reading Comprehension	*Writing*

- **Peabody Individual Achievement Test-Revised**

Dunn, L. M. & Markwardt, F. C. (1989). *Peabody individual achievement test-Revised.* Circle Pines, MN: American Guidance Service.

This is the most commonly used individually administered achievement test in special education for identifying academic strengths and difficulties. It is intended for students 5 years old through adulthood and may take up to 60 minutes to administer. Each of the sections are presented in a multiple-choice format in which the student can respond by pointing or saying the correct answer. PIAT-R scores include age- and grade- based standard scores, age and grade equivalents, and percentile ranks and stanines for all subjects except written expression.

Relevant sections of this test include:

Reading Recognition	*Spelling*
Reading Comprehension	*Written Expression*

- **Woodcock Diagnostic Reading Battery**

Woodcock, R. W. (1997). *Woodcock diagnostic reading battery.* Riverside, CA: The Riverside Publishing Co.

This is an individually administered test used to measure ten aspects of reading achievement, as well as a set of closely related abilities. The Woodcock is used to diagnose strengths and difficulties in five areas: basic reading skills, reading comprehension, phonological awareness, oral-language comprehension, and reading aptitude. The test is appropriate for instructional planning, including the development of IEPs, and can be used to monitor the progress of students over the school year. Subtests include:

Letter-Word Identification	*Listening Comprehension*
Word Attack	*Memory for Sentences*
Reading Vocabulary	*Visual Matching*
Passage Comprehension	*Oral Vocabulary*
Incomplete Words	*Sound Blending*

- **Test of Written Language-3**

Hammill, D. D. & Larsen, S. (1996). *Test of written language (3rd edition).* Austin, TX: Pro-Ed Inc.

This is an individually administered, norm-referenced device designed to assess written-language competence of students ages 7-18. The test has two written formats (contrived and spontaneous) to evaluate written language. In the contrived format, student's linguistic options are purposely constrained to force them to use specific words or conventions of the English language. In the spontaneous format, students respond to a picture as a story starter. Three components of written language are assessed by these two formats: The Conventional Component deals with using the rules of Standard American English in spelling, capitalization, and punctuation. The Linguistic Component deals with syntactic and semantic structures, and the Cognitive Component deals with producing logical, coherent, and sequenced written products. Subtests to elicit writing in contrived contexts include:

Vocabulary	*Sentence Combining*
Spelling	*Logical Sentences*
Style	

Subtests to elicit writing in spontaneous contexts include:

Contextualized Conventions	*Story Construction*
Contextualized Language	

Teachers who desire more information on assessing students with disabilities should consult the following:

Bos, C.S. & Vaughn, S (1998). *Stategies for teaching students with learningand behavior problems.* (4th Ed.). Boston: Allyn and Bacon.

Lipson, M. Y., & Wixson, K. K. (1997). *Assessment & instruction of reading and writing disability: An interactive approach (2nd Ed.).* New York: Longman.

Morrow, L. M. (1993). *Literacy development in the early years: Helping children read and write (2nd Ed.).* Boston: Allyn and Bacon.

Polloway, E. A., & Patton, J. R. (1997). *Strategies for teaching learners with special needs (6th Ed.).* Upper Saddle River, New Jersey: Merrill/Prentice Hall.

Part Three

Teaching Word Identification and Comprehension
Strategies to Students with Mental Retardation

What is reading?

Reading, like riding a bike can be described as a highly
complex and multifaceted human behavior. For example, a
person first learning to ride a bike must concentrate on
mastering specific skills such as pedaling, steering,
balancing, turning, and stopping the bike so as not to fall.
Later, with greater proficiency, bike riding becomes more of
a natural, integrated, and holistic act. Similarly, reading is
also characterized by specific isolated skills, such as
discriminating letters, identifying words, and understanding
specific vocabulary—and, like bike riding, should become
an equally integrated, natural, and holistic act. Performing
the separate subskills in isolation does not constitute
proficiency in either bike riding or reading.

The goal of reading is to derive meaning from text. To
achieve comprehension, readers must interact with
passages using word identification strategies, self-
questioning strategies, and background knowledge. A
reading program must include instruction in
comprehension strategies because word identification
alone does not support reading comprehension. For
example, Jacob focuses solely on identifying words in a
reading passage and believes he is "reading", yet does not
have any understanding of what he has "read." Mary
reads but does not draw on her background knowledge
and has difficulty answering questions. These students
must be taught how new knowledge can be acquired from
reading. They must understand how to use strategies to
organize, categorize, and associate new knowledge with
previously learned information.

What Must Teachers Know About the English Language to Teach Reading?

Several important terms, concepts, and ideas are discussed in this section to facilitate the planning and instruction of reading and writing to students with mental retardation. Teachers are encouraged to become familiar with these concepts for effective literacy instruction.

- **Metalinguistics**- refers to student's awareness about language and its use. Students learn that language is an object that can be talked about, thought about, and manipulated. One of the key aspects of metalinguistics is student's learning sound-symbol relationships and its application to reading. They must be taught that meaning or ideas can be segmented into words, and that words can be broken-down into syllables and individual sounds (phonemes). For example, the word bat has three separate phonemes (/b/ /a/ /t/). Research indicates that the following skills are necessary for successful acquisition of early reading:
  -**Segmentation**- dividing ideas into words, and words into syllables and phonemes.
  -**Phonemic analysis**- analyzing parts of words into phonemes or speech sounds.
  -**Blending**- putting the sounds or phonemes together to form words.

Unfortunately, substantial evidence exists to suggest that students with learning problems are deficient in this segmentation, phonemic analysis, and blending.

Other important and useful methods or strategies that assist skilled readers to identify words in a passage include the following.

- **Word Configuration Clues**- This is an outline of the general shape of a word. Word length, uppercase letters, and letter height can provide some visual cues to the reader. Think about the letters b,d,p,q. Each consists of a ball and a stick. The stick may go above the line as in b and d or below the line in p and q. Experienced readers use the shape of letters and words to aid in identification.

- **Semantic Clues**- This means using the words in the text and the meaning of the text to help identify words. When teachers ask "What word makes sense?", we are asking students to use semantic clues and his or her semantic knowledge. For example, in the sentence "The boy went to the store to get a loaf of _____." A student who is able to apply semantic clues to figure-out the word that goes in the blank would know that "bread" is the most meaningful answer.

- **Syntactic Clues**- This means using knowledge of grammatical information to assist in identifying an unknown word. In the sentence, "Carlos rode his _____ down the street", the reader knows that the word in the blank must be a noun. The combination of using semantic clues and syntactic clues is termed usage of context clues. For example, in the following two sentences the italicized word is spelled the same way, but has two very different pronunciations and meanings. "The wind blew over the table." Please wind up the toy and make it go." Context allows readers to identify and understand the words.

- **Structural Analysis**- This is the use of meaningful units such as root words (act in the words action, react, transact, actor, enact), prefixes (anti, auto, dis), suffixes (tion, ed), possessives, plurals, word families, and compound words.

- **Phonics Analysis**- This is phonics, and it involves decoding words by their sound-symbol relationship. Students must recognize graphemes (symbols such as vowels and consonants) and pronounce the corresponding phoneme (sound). Some basic phonetic concepts teachers should know:
  -**Long vowels**- Long vowels say their own name as does the letter "a" in the words "ape" and "gate".

-Short vowels- Short vowels take on a different sound as does the letter "a" in the words "apple" and "pal".

-Consonant blends- Consonant blends are two consecutive letters where each has its own phoneme, as in "bl" in the word "blend".

-Consonant clusters- Consonant clusters are three successive letters where each has its own phoneme, as in "spl" in the word "splash".

-Digraphs- Digraphs are two successive letters whose phonetic value is a single sound as in the vowel digraph "ea" in the word "bread"; or the consonant digraph "ch" as in the word "church".

How Can Teachers Help Students Recognize Words and Improve Comprehension?

To successfully aid students in word identification and reading comprehension, teachers have numerous resources and techniques available from which to choose. Teachers need to determine each student's developmental level in literacy so that appropriate instruction can be planned. It is also suggested that the presentation of materials be conducted in small groups, rather than individually. This instructional format allows proficient readers to model and assist less capable readers to improve their skills. The following strategies are provided to improve word identification and comprehension skills.

• **The Classroom Library Center (All Levels)**
The purpose of the classroom library is to give students an opportunity to gain competence interacting with books of their own choosing, to develop more conventional concepts about print, facilitate positive attitudes about books, and develop independent reading skills. The classroom library should contain children's literature that includes theme books, storybooks, fairy tales, picture books, alphabet books, fables, holiday books, and trade books.

Students visit the classroom library center daily, working under the guidance of an adult. Each time they are instructed to select a book to be "read" alone, to another student, or to an adult. From the beginning of the school year students are guided to select and interact with books. Modeling and reinforcing conventional book interactions for students (holding the book properly, turning pages, starting to read at the top of the page, etc.) teaches them these behaviors. In their reading selection, students are encouraged to attempt to determine what the story is about and the events to occur. This is accomplished by looking at the pictures and words, and recalling from memory what they remember about the story. Students can be paired as partners so that more conventional readers model literacy skills for less conventional readers.

The teacher's role is to observe and record each student's book selection and identify how they use the book during a specific interaction. An observation system developed by Martinez and Teale (1988), include the following type of student interactions. The lowest level is ***browsing*** where students rapidly flip through the pages of a book, thus requiring the least amount of sustained attention. The intermediate level is ***silent studying*** where students slowly turn the pages of a storybook and purposely view and study specific text and/or pictures without discussion or portrayal. Finally, the highest level is ***independent reenactments*** where students verbally reenact some or all elements of a story by using picture, memory readings, or printed text. Reenactments, ranging from picture-governed to print-governed attempts, can be performed alone, with a partner, or within a group.

- **Guided Story Telling (Preconventional, Emergent)**
  Guided story telling is a reading activity that involves listening, thinking, speaking, and paying attention by following a story sequence using only pictures. Its purpose is to develop background knowledge, facilitate listening,

develop vocabulary and oral language skills, and teach students to use picture and context clues to determine story meaning. It also helps develop student's sense of "storiness"; the idea that there is a structure to a narrative story such as characters, a sequence of events, a problem, and a resolution of the problem. The pictures in stories play an important role in supporting student's understanding and construction of meaning from the pages in books.

Guided Story Telling revolves around books which contain few, if any words, but are rich in pictures. For example, the three books, *Good Dog, Carl; Carl Goes Shopping;* and *Carl's Christmas*, by Alexandria Day, each have a short amount of text at the beginning meant to be read aloud by an adult, with only pictures on the remaining pages. Students should be prompted to talk about and describe the story action on each page. With experience and support by the teacher, students will eventually be able to "weave" a coherent, sequentially accurate story across pages using only picture clues (Katims, 1996).

- **The Logo Poster (Preconventional, Emergent)**

The purpose of the logo poster activity is to show students that print in any form is meaningful. The use of environmental print in beginning reading instruction may help students understand the function and forms of print, increase letter-name awareness and metalinguistic ability. Most importantly, it provides them the understanding that they can be **readers**. The logo poster consists of a number of commercial pictures and logos from the community environment. The numerous logos pasted on the poster board may include: "Coca-Cola", "McDonald's", "Toys 'R' Us", "Burger King", "Peter Pan" peanut butter, "Crayola", "K-Mart", "Sears", "Jell-O", "Kellogg's", and so on. Students take turns "reading" and talking daily about the logos on the board. They come to understand that if they can "read" the logos, they are in fact really "reading". This theme, used in combination with other literacy activities, can help students fully grasp the idea that the purpose of reading is to understand the message of the author.

- ### The Language Experience Approach (Emergent, Early, Developing, Fluent)

  The purpose of the language experience approach is to teach students about written language and how to read and write within the context of their own dictated stories. Typically, students engage in a common experience such as a field trip to the zoo or circus, baking cookies, or taking a walk. Students take turns dictating sentences to the teacher who prints their responses on a flipchart. The written story becomes the basis of each student's reading instruction. Students are asked to "read" the story after the teacher reads it aloud. The story is copied by each student and used for individual or group mini-lessons.

  Objectives of the mini-lessons include learning the letters of the alphabet, understanding the relation of letters and words, learning that language is made up of words, syllable, and phonemes, learning letter sounds, learning to sound out new words, word identification and comprehension strategies, punctuation, grammar instruction, and so on. The Cloze technique, as well as flashcards and sentence strips are used to teach important concepts and ideas contained in the story. These important skills are taught within the context of a connected text developed by the students.

- ### The Daily News Flash (All levels)

  The daily news flash is an exercise similar to the common Language Experience Approach described above. Each school day begins with the oral language activity called "the daily news flash". Students are encouraged to talk freely about important events and occurrences in their lives. The purpose of the daily news flash is to foster mutual respect, the ability to listen and respond to one another, develop background knowledge, develop vocabulary and oral language skills, and help students attend to the graphophonic, semantic and syntactic clues of their news story in written form.

Each day a student's news item is printed on a flipchart as they speak. Students are directed to use various word identification strategies to read their own story. This experiential approach to teaching initial reading and word identification strategies capitalizes on the linguistic, cognitive, social, and cultural knowledge of each student so that the transfer from oral language to written language can be made. Reading becomes personally meaningful to each student with this approach.

A typical "daily news flash" might be from a 4th grade student named Juanita, with moderate mental retardation. For example in January, as Juanita spoke, it was recorded on the classroom flipchart: "My Grandma is coming to see me on my birthday. I love to be with my Grandma." She is then asked to come to the flipchart to locate and circle her name and underline specific letters and words she recognizes. Words, phrases, and sentences from dictated news flash stories are printed on wordcards, sentence strips and the chalkboard, to be used for direct instruction throughout the school day. Juanita and other students are provided instruction in matching sentence strips and wordcards against the text of dictated stories, and asked to arranged them in correct sequence.

Figure 3.1
Example of a Daily News Flash

January 2000
Daily News Flash
Juanita

My Grandma is coming to see me on my birthday.

I love to be with my Grandma.

- **Group Storybook Reading Using Predicable Books, Sentence Strips and Word Cards (All Levels)**

Teachers should read aloud to their students daily. Multiple readings of storybooks has shown to encourage wide-ranging exploration of books by students and to promote emergent and fluent reading behaviors. The purpose of daily storybook readings is to facilitate literacy through exposure to the language and pictures found in high quality children's books. This activity helps students develop listening and specific reading skills, such as sight word vocabulary, semantic and syntactic analysis.

Teachers systematically introduce individual books by reading them aloud to students. We now know that students without disabilities, as well as students with disabilities, interact in more sophisticated ways with *familiar books*. Teachers attempt to make many books familiar to students through multiple readings. The expectation is that familiar books will encourage interactions with books and aid in the development of language competence believed to be vital to producing basic beginning literacy behaviors.

The availability of *predictable books* has also been shown to affect student's responses to stories. Books and stories considered "predictable" are those containing rhythmical and/or repetitive patterns that make it easy for early readers to begin predicting what will be on the page. Predictable books afford students a special kind of access because their predictable features directly aid, facilitate, and encourage them to reconstruct the story independently. For example, the repetitious verse of Bill Martin's, "Brown Bear, Brown Bear, what do you see, I see a _____ looking at me", readily encourages students to help the teacher read the book. A list of predictable books may be found in the reference section at the end of this monograph.

Bos and Vaughn (1998) suggest the following procedure for teachers to use in group storybook readings:

1. Read the book aloud to the students. Reread the book,

inviting the students to join in when they can predict what will come next. Have the students take turns choral reading (reading in unison).

2. Put the text of the book on a large flipchart without the book's picture cues. Read and choral read the story from the chart. Give the students sentence strips with sentences from the story. Have them match the sentence strips to the chart and then read the sentences.

3. Give the students individual word cards from the story, in order. Have the students place each card under the matching word on the chart.

4. Read and choral read the story from the chart. Place the individual word cards from sections of the story in random order, at the bottom of the chart. Have the students match the word cards to the words in the story.

- **Group Storybook Reading with Story Maps for Student Retellings (Early, Developing, Fluent)**

Group storybook readings can also be used in combination with story retellings by students in order to increase their listening and reading comprehension. Teachers provide visual and verbal prompts to support students in their retelling of stories that are read aloud. The purpose of retelling a story offers active participation in a literacy experience that helps a student develop language structures, comprehension, and a sense of story structure. Story maps are visual representations of narrative texts, which aid students in retelling the story by structuring responses. These maps provide students with a visual guide for understanding and retelling stories, while adults prompt and direct student's retellings. This technique leads to better understanding of the story.

For example, a teacher reads aloud a familiar book from the classroom library (selected by a student). They choose one or more students to retell the story using a large story map poster that contains visual prompts for the various parts of narrative stories. The teacher prompts with questions pertaining to, "Where did this story take place?", "Who was the main character in this story?", "Were there other characters in this story?" What kind of problem did the main character have?", "What happened first in this story, then next, and then last?", "What was the solution to the problem?" Figure 3.2 is an example of a story map available for teachers to use in the classroom.

Figure 3.2

Example of a Story Map

Name of Story_____

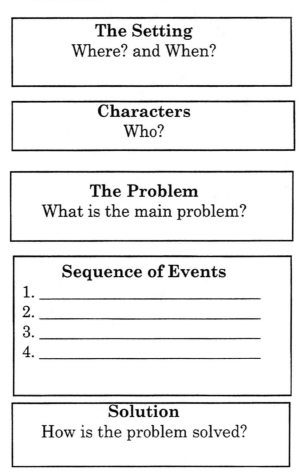

- **Group Storybook Reading with the Predictive Cycle (Emergent, Early, Developing)**

A three-phase sampling, predicting, and confirming cycle can be used in conjunction with group storybook reading. Tompkins and Webeler (1983) believe that beginning readers can use the three-step cycle while listening to familiar and predictable books read aloud by the teacher. The purpose of the predictive cycle is to prompt and support students in constructing important predictions about stories, eventually leading to higher levels of independent interactions with books.

-**Sampling**- The teacher begins by reading aloud a familiar story to the students who sample the words and pictures on the page of the book (The Three Bears, for example).

-**Predicting**- The teacher prompts the students to make a prediction about what they think will happen on a particular page by listening carefully and observing the pictures (for example, when Baby Bear and Mama Bear each say "Somebody has been sleeping in my bed." The teacher asks "What will happen next?").

-**Confirming**- The students listening carefully as the teacher turns the page and reads the text aloud to see if their prediction is correct, confirming their developing ability to predict what will happen next.

- **Basal Readers (Early, Developing, Fluent)**

More advanced students can engage in reading a contemporary basal reader, or other connected texts. Contemporary basal readers (for example, MacMillan/ McGraw-Hill Reading/Language Arts series offers an excellent contemporary basal series), consist of high quality children's literature instead of the stilted and controlled vocabulary of the old-fashioned basals (such as the old Dick and Jane series). Students can also read trade books, newspapers, or any other appropriate reading material.

The purpose of using basal readers and other connected texts is similar to activities previously mentioned. Students can be given direct instruction in each of the word identification strategies, comprehension enhancement, and fluency. Teachers have the option to have students read aloud together in unison (choral reading), read in pairs with one student reading to another while the other follows along in the text, and reversing roles every other page (paired reading), and/or students reading individually. The purpose of this activity includes teaching the use of sight words, phonics strategies, and other decoding skills, and to guide comprehension activities before, during, and after reading (Hedrick, Katims, and Carr, 1999).

The teacher directs comprehension activities. They introduce and build background information for the text, set specific goals for reading, and complete follow- up activities. After reading the text, the group can complete a comprehension activity collectively, not individually. For example, the teacher might direct the students to read in order to determine the chronological order of events. After the students have read the text, the teacher might copy several major events from the text onto the board placed out of sequence. The task of the students as a group is to organize events into correct sequence. Using story retelling with a story map is also an appropriate and useful follow-up activity.

- **Working With Words (Early, Developing, Fluent)**

Students who are more conventionally literate can work on decoding skills using isolated word work that focuses on sight words and manipulation of phonetic elements. The purpose of this activity is twofold: To familiarize students with highly regular phonetic patterns using "Making Words" and with high frequency sight words using a "Word Wall".

"Making Words" is an activity in which decoding skills are supported by the manipulation of letters into words. In this activity developed by Cunningham and Cunningham (1992), students use 6-9 cut-up alphabet letters at their desk to "make" words as the teacher dictates them. The teacher begins by calling out 2-letter words, then 3-letter words, etc., until the last word called out requires each student to "make" a "big" word using all the letters on their desk. For example, in the big word "parrots", students are asked to make 2-letter words ("or', "at"); make 3-letter words ("rot", "rat"), and so on until they can spell the word "parrots". Once all the words have been "made", the students sort the words in a variety of ways. She may request the students to sort the words by looking at the first letter or perhaps by finding the words that contain the same spelling pattern such as -"-at, -or".

"Word Wall" activities provide students with varied opportunities to interact with high frequency words displayed on the wall in the front of the classroom. At the beginning of the week the teacher introduces 3-4 new words for the wall. Words are selected that are high frequency and may have irregular spelling patterns, such as "the", "a", and "what". These words are arranged according to vowels as illustrated in Figure 3.3 (Adams, 1990).

Figure 3.3

An Example of a Word Wall

a	e	i	o	u
gate	eaten	bit	fabulous	fun
tar	dread	like	skeleton	fur
	her	tonight		bubble

The teacher then calls out words as the students write them on paper. This activity can be described as an "open book" spelling test. The teacher does a variety of activities using the words on the wall in addition to the daily spelling test. For example, one activity might have students take turns reading the words out loud in alphabetically order, as they "look" at the words on the wall. Students also enjoy being timed to determine if they can read all the words on the wall in less time than the day before.

- **Rimes and Onsets (Early, Developing, Fluent)**

This activity goes hand-in-hand with the word wall activity described above. The purposes are the same as well. The teacher uses rimes, which are consistent and reliable word families to help students gain knowledge of, and competence with word patterns. A typical example of a rime is the "at" family. Once a student can pronounce or write this rime, they are able to make a large number of words by adding various on-sets. Examples include, r-at, c-at, m-at, s-at, and so on—to adding consonant blends and clusters, fl-at, spl-at, and so on. In her book, Adams (1990) cites evidence that only 37 rimes make up approximately 500 primary grade words (See Figure 3.4).

Figure 3.4

Common Rimes (Word Families)

Common Rimes (word families)					
ack	ank	eat	ill	ock	ump
ail	ap	ell	in	oke	unk
ain	ash	est	ine	op	
ake	at	ice	ing	ore	
ale	ate	ick	ink	ot	
ame	aw	ide	ip	uck	
an	ay	ight	it	ug	

- **Brainstorming (Early, Developing, Fluent)**

Brainstorming is an effective instructional tool conducted prior to reading that activates relevant prior knowledge important to effective and efficient processing of information. It also stimulates interest in a topic to be read and helps the teacher identify the extent of the student's background knowledge (Bos & Vaughn, 1998). An extension activity to brainstorming is the use of a follow-up activity after reading a story. According to Bos and Vaughn, the strategy works best with groups of students reading the same selection. Teachers must first determine the major topic or concept presented in the selection (for example, a passage about sharks), and then decide what to use as a stimulus to represent that topic (the word *shark*, or *man-eater*, or *Great White* is printed on the board, or a picture of a shark is used). The following outline is presented as a guide:

1. Present the word, phrase or picture to the students.
2. Ask the students to list or say as many words or phrases as they can associate with the original word, phrase or picture. Encourage them to think about everything they know about the topic. Allow several minutes for the students to think, write, and get ready to report their ideas.
3. Record their associations on the board. Ask for other associations and add them to the list.
4. The teacher and students draw a concept map, word web, or simply list their responses into categories (habitats, food, movies, etc.).
5. Have students read the selected story as you believe is appropriate for the group—either verbally, taking turns, or silently.
6. After the selection has been read, ask the students for further associations with the original word, phrase, or picture. The ideas that come now should be much more elaborate, rich, and robust.

• **K-W-L (Early, Developing, Fluent)**

A fairly sophisticated activity which may be completed before, during and after reading a text, is the K-W-L technique. Ogle, (1986) designed the K-W-L procedure for increasing reading comprehension. The purpose of this three-step cognitive procedure is to help students recognize prior knowledge, predict new types of information to be acquired from reading, and review what is learned from reading:

K- What I know. The student writes down, dictates, or talks about prior knowledge regarding the topic to read (sharks, for example).

W- What I want to learn. The student anticipates or predicts what will be learned about the topic of the selection and writes it down, dictates it, or talks about it.

L- What I learned. The student writes down, dictates, or talks about what he or she learned from reading the selection.

Teachers can vary the K-W-L approach by using the technique where students follow along with them as they model the K-W-L steps while "thinking aloud" and reading a selection. Once students understand the process, teachers can provide students with a selection to read alone and use a K-W-L chart. A primary focus of using the K-W-L chart is to teach students to self-talk/think about what they are reading in order to improve comprehension. Table 3.5 is an example of K-W-L chart:

Figure 3.5

K-W-L Chart

Name _____ Date _____

KWL CHART

WHAT I KNOW	WHAT I WANT To Find Out	WHAT I LEARNED

Teachers who desire more information on how to teach word recognition and comprehension strategies to students with disabilities should consult the following:

Bos, C. S., & Vaughn, S. (1998). *Strategies for teaching students with learningand behavior problems (4th Ed.).* Boston: Allyn and Bacon.

Cunningham, P. M., & Cunningham, J. W. (1992). *Making words: Enhancing the invented spelling-decoding connection.* The Reading Teacher, 46, 106-116.

Mercer, C. D., & Mercer, A. R. (1998). *Teaching students with learning problems (5th Ed.).* Upper Saddle River, New Jersey: Merrill/Prentice Hall.

Polloway, E. A., & Patton, J. R. (1997). *Strategies for teaching learners with special needs (6th Ed.).* Upper Saddle River, New Jersey: Merrill/Prentice Hall.

Thomas, G. E. (1996). *Teaching students with mental retardation: A life goal curriculum planning approach.* Upper Saddle River, New Jersey: Merrill/Prentice Hall.

Wood, K. D., & Algozzine, B. (1994). *Teaching reading to high-risk learners: A unified approach.* Boston: Allyn and Bacon.

Teaching Writing Strategies to Students with Mental Retardation

What is Writing?

Reading and writing are complimentary activities. Readers reconstruct text by constructing meaning; writers reconstruct meaning by constructing text. Reading and writing abilities reinforce one another, so they must be taught concurrently and interrelatedly, rather than sequentially, thus providing opportunities for students to "write" about useful and meaningful events and topics. Teachers should always aim to combine both reading and writing activities as often as possible.

One of the ways of introducing writing to early level students can be accomplished by modeling and displaying a poster depicting the five major forms of "writing". These five forms illustrate the developmental stages that students progressively achieve (Sulzby, 1989):

- **Writing via Drawing**- The student draws a picture for the entire composition or embeds pictures within other forms of writing to represent words and ideas.
- **Writing via Scribbling**- The student uses continuous and/or noncontinuous curvy or pointed horizontal forms of scribble to represent words or ideas.
- **Writing via Letter Strings**- The student uses either random or patterned letters to represent words or ideas.
- **Writing via Invented Spelling**- The student uses phonetic relationships between sounds in spoken words and letters expressing those words. Partial invented spellings use a letter for some of the syllables contained in a word, such as "*wt*" for "*want*"; full invented spelling uses a letter for all, or almost all, of the sounds in the spoken word, such as "*mothr*" for "*mother*").

- **Writing via Conventional Spelling**- At this stage students are able to write words with conventional spelling such as "dog', "cat", "mom", and so on.

At every opportunity possible, students should be encouraged and supported in their attempts to "write" in order to relay a meaningful message (as opposed to tracing or copying letters in isolation). The purpose of initial writing activities is to eventually develop in students what Clay (1975) calls the **generative principle**—understanding that the writer can create new meanings by reorganizing a limited set of units, particularly the letters of the alphabet. Given this idea, students can share their "writings" by "reading" them aloud to other students to show various developing forms of writing.

How Do Students with Mental Retardation Progress in Writing?

Evidence shows that students with mental retardation progress through the five major forms of writing as described above (Hedrick, Katims, & Carr, 1999; Katims, 1991). One investigation involved elementary students with mild to moderate levels of mental retardation (Katims, 1996). Students were provided direction and instruction in their "writing" throughout the school year by use of several techniques described in this part of the monograph. In the first period of the study (September though January), students used different forms of "writing" modeled by the teacher. With practice, modeling, feedback, and teacher encouragement, students displayed more conventional forms of "writing" with regularity during the second period of the study (February through May). Writing samples of each of the four students were analyzed by use of an expanded writing scheme developed by Sulzby (1989). The results are shown in Table 4.1.

Table 4.1

Progression of Writing Behaviors Over the School Year (Expressed as Percentages)

Classification of Writing	Maria		Rose		Alma		Joseph	
	1	2	1	2	1	2	1	2
Drawing	52	41	11	5	6	4	47	32
Scribble-wavy	12	10	9	4	2	1	13	8
Scribble-letter-like	8	7	8	6	3	1	9	6
Letter-like units	4	5	8	15	7	5	4	5
Letters-random	5	9	5	8	14	4	3	9
Letters-patterns	2	7	10	19	19	9	1	8
Letters-elements	4	6	7	8	2	1	2	6
Environmental copying	12	10	37	18	26	29	21	18
Invented spelling-partial	1	2	4	9	14	18	0	5
Invented spelling-full	0	1	1	3	5	21	0	2
Conventional writing	0	2	0	5	2	7	0	1

1 = September -January. 2 = February-May.

Notice that during the first period of the study, students frequently used less conventional forms of writing. As the school year progressed, they used more and more conventional forms of writing. Although few students consistently used conventional writing, they began to use letters (in various forms), environmental copying, and even invented spellings to express themselves on everyday writing tasks.

A primary goal for teachers providing instruction in written communication skills is to create a classroom community writing environment. The writing community allows students to view other students contemplating and working on written language in various forms. Students are also able to observe teachers performing various writing tasks such as writing notes, writing on the chalkboard, writing labels for cubbies and storage shelves in the classroom, and grading papers.

How Can Teachers Help Students Improve Their Expressive Writing?

Described below are techniques that teachers utilize to introduce and instruct students to improve their written communication skills. Each technique has been successfully used with students who have mild to moderate levels of mental retardation.

- **The Classroom Writing Center (Preconventional, Emergent, Early)**

  The Classroom Writing Center is a place specifically designated for writing activities. The center needs to be accessible, attractive, and inviting to all students. Items that create a comfortable environment are furnishings such as sofas, chairs, beanbag chairs, a large table, and carpet squares. Also, an ample variety of writing supplies need to be readily accessible to students, such as pencils (large, small and colored), pens, markers, and paper. Students should be invited to work in the classroom writing center several times a week throughout the school year. Purposes for visiting the writing center are to have students "write" about books that were recently read to them, or interacted with independently, or to write about other real-life topics of interest, including holiday greetings, birthday cards, messages, seasonal themes, and everyday, meaningful events.

  The classroom writing center is introduced the first day of the school year so that children view themselves as "writers" from the start. Students are taught that the purpose of writing is to convey meaning. Even though not everyone will be able to read everything they write, if it has meaning to them, it is writing. Whenever children visit the writing center they are encouraged to "write" (never to draw or color), and the teacher should accept all attempts to do so as "writing", regardless of the type of scribble or mark. Questions always should be posed to students such as— "what does it say?", "What did you write?" (See Katims & Pierce, 1995). With much direction and practice students begin to progress in their ability to express themselves in more conventional forms of writing.

- **Picture Writing (Preconventional, Emergent, Early)**

  The purposes of the picture writing strategy are to facilitate student's understanding of what writing is all about, as well as to develop student's ability to express themselves in writing. The procedure involves asking students to first draw a picture, or cut a picture out of a magazine, and paste it on a piece of paper. Then students are encouraged to discuss their picture with a partner or adult volunteer, and then to "write" about their picture. In this exercise, some students will use invented spellings, and others will write correctly spelled words, sentences, phrases, or even paragraphs. Mini-lessons can be conducted so that teachers use a student's written product for instruction in creating more conventional written messages.

  Figure 4.1 is an example of a writing book developed by Norma Carr, a veteran teacher of students with mental retardation in San Antonio, Texas. She directs her emergent and early literate students to draw a picture on the top of the page and "write" about the picture at the bottom of the page. The book itself has colored paper as the cover and is stapled with 20 or 30 sheets of paper. A line is drawn through the middle of each page.

Figure 4.1

My Writing Book

- **A Structured Writing Lesson (Emergent, Early, Developing)**

  In this activity, the teacher conducts a mini-writing lesson while modeling a writing "think aloud" strategy for the students. For example, teachers self-question themselves aloud as a model for students. Teachers ask themselves questions such as: "what word can I put in the blank to make sense?" "Did I sound-out all of the parts of the word?" The purpose of the writing lesson is to support students in their efforts to get their thoughts down on paper, so others can read what they have written. A secondary purpose is to reinforce reading skills such as metalinguistic ability, letter/sound relationships, and understanding concepts about print. Teachers create sentences so that they can capture personal responses from each student.

For example, a teacher may write on the board "I like ____ for lunch." The students would receive assistance in reading the words and then engage in a dialogue about the possibilities of food items they like for lunch. Each child copies the sentence and fills in the blank with a personal answer. Students can also fill in missing words from predictable books they are familiar with such as, "Brown Bear, _____ _____, what do you ____, I see a _____ looking at me." Over time, the structure is lessened (faded) so that the teacher might print a question on the board for students to answer, such as "What is your favorite game to play after school?" Or, a verbal cue could be given such as "Describe an apple" (see Hedrick, Katims, & Carr, 1999).

- **Journal Writing (Early, Developing, Fluent)**

Teachers can encourage and inspire written communication by the use of writing journals. Each student is provided a small spiral notebook or a stack of notebook paper stapled together, with the student's name printed on the front cover. Students make daily entries in their personal journal. Students are encouraged to write at their own developmental level. Thus, some journals include only drawings, scribbles, random letters, or invented spelling. The teacher models journal writing by printing a personal message on the board such as, "I am really excited today. My new eyeglasses are ready for me." Or by asking students to draw a picture of something they participated in over the weekend and label the different parts in the picture. By having students make regular entries in their journal, teachers can record individual progress over time to share with parents.

• **Working with Sentences (Early, Developing, Fluent)**

Mercer and Mercer (1998) provide a number of recommendations for students with disabilities that are appropriate for students with mild to moderate mental retardation. These are activities that might be called working with sentences because they provide students practice with real sentences.

- Provide scrambled words from a sentence and ask the students to arrange the words to form sentences:

  her quietly cat the food ate

  friends yesterday Jane's left

- List several words and have students write a sentence that contains all the words:

puppy	my	I
school	bring	to
to	would	like

- Have students complete partial sentences written on the board. Gradually decrease the number of words presented:

  Yesterday morning the dog barked at . . .

  Yesterday morning the dog . . .

  Yesterday morning . . .

- Provide various noun and verb phrases and have students expand each sentence by adding descriptive words:

man ate	The man in blue shirt ate his dinner slowly.
dog barked	The big, black dog barked at the maN with the stick.

- Have the students combine related sentences into one sentence:

The policeman is Young	The young policemen stopped the car.

  The policemen stopped the car.

| Yesterday the boys played a football game. The game lasted two hours. | Yesterday the boys played a football game that lasted two hours. |

- **Using a Prompt Technique (Early, Developing, Fluent)**

Schloss, Harriman, and Pfiefer (1985) developed a technique for writers with disabilities that is also appropriate for students with mild to moderate mental retardation. A modification of their procedure is presented below:

1. Present (or elicit from the student) a topic for the student to write about (sharks).
2. Encourage the student to vocalize each sentence before writing it.
3. Tell the student that assistance in spelling will be provided if requested.
4. Wait 20 seconds after announcing the topic for the student to **self-initiate** a sentence aloud.
5. If a sentence is not vocalized and written after 20 seconds, provide a **motivational prompt**, urging the student to begin writing (e.g., "Go ahead and do your best.").
6. If a sentence is not vocalized and written after another 20 seconds, provide a **content prompt**, giving the general content of an appropriate sentence (e.g., "Write about how a shark catches fish.").
7. If a sentence is not produced after a third, 20-second period, provide a **literal prompt** to the student that tells precisely what to write (e.g., "Write 'the shark chased the fish into shallow water.' ").
8. As soon as student writes the sentence, return to the **self-initiated prompt** level and repeat the sequence as needed until the composition is complete.

9. Provide feedback to the student as to how many sentences were self-initiated, and the number that were produced under each prompt level.

- **Experience Stories and Charts (Early, Developing, Fluent)**

  Using experience stories for writing instruction is similar to the Language Experience Approach described earlier. One major purpose of this approach for beginning writers is to teach them to organize ideas as a precursor to writing them down on paper. When using experience charts and stories, sentences should be short, and vocabulary should be kept simple. A small number of sentences should be used, but each should contribute significantly to the story. Words should be repeated throughout the story to familiarize students with their spelling and use. Schloss and Sedlak (1986) recommend the following sequence for creating and using an experience chart:

  1. Select a topic to be used (i.e., planning a trip, a picture, summer activities).
  2. Discuss the topic with the students.
  3. Elicit a title for the story through a series of questions to the students.
  4. Print or write the title on a chart or board large enough for all to see.
  5. In early stories, each sentence should be only one line long.
  6. Have students contribute sentences to the story through the use of teacher initiated questions. The teacher writes or prints the sentences students dictate.
  7. Read the story aloud after it is completed.
  8. Have the students read the story aloud and copy it on their paper.

- **Sequential Writing Instruction (Emergent, Early, Developing, Fluent)**

This approach is designed for emergent, early, developing and fluent writers in that as students gain the experience, confidence, and ability to express themselves in more sophisticated ways, the degree of teacher support for writing is reduced. Figure 4.2 is a modification of an idea originally presented by Kameenui and Simmons (1990). Beginning writers are prompted to write words (as best they can and using invented spellings) as the result of being stimulated by a single picture (drawn by the teacher, students, cut from a magazine, or any other source). More advanced writers are stimulated with multiple pictures and asked to write sentences. Even more conventional students are stimulated to write paragraphs and stories with the use of topic sentences, or a single topic written on the board by the teacher.

Figure 4.2

Instructional Variations for Expressive Writing Practice

Variable	Beginning Writing Instruction		Advanced Writing Instruction	
Degree of teacher guidance	Extensive————————> Minimal (Faded as students demonstrate competence)			
Instructional tools	Single picture -->	Multiple pictures -->	Topic sentence -->	Topic
Written product	Words -->	Sentences-->		Paragraphs

- **A Writing Planning Sheet (Developing, Fluent)**

Some teachers structure writing experiences by using a writing planning sheet. The purpose of the planning sheet is to support, scaffold and structure student's writing efforts as they develop their ability to express themselves independently. The planning sheet helps organize the student's thinking processes about writing, and structures their responses. As time goes on, the structure of the sheet can be eliminated and students may be able to write with verbal prompts from the teacher, and eventually take on the writing task independently. An example of a general think sheet is illustrated in Figure 4.3.

Figure 4.3

A Writing Planning Sheet

A WRITING PLANNING SHEET

Topic _____

What do I know about this topic?
1.
2.
3.
4.
How can I organize my ideas?
Title _____
Topic Sentence _____
_____
Supporting detail 1 _____
_____
Supporting detail 2 _____
_____
Supporting detail 3 _____
_____
Summary Statement _____
_____

- **Story Starters (Emergent, Early, Developing, Fluent)**

The purpose of using a story starter is to help students begin to put their ideas down on paper by stimulating their interest and ideas. The use of story starters involves the teacher providing students with a beginning sentence or idea to write about, or respond to. Teachers can use a recent field trip, a current event, or any common experience to stimulate their students to begin to write. Examples include:

The food in our cafeteria is "yucky" because . . . .

Saturday morning I usually like to. . .

If I were President of the United States I would . . .

Once students begin to get their ideas down on paper, they are encouraged to talk and think about ideas they may want to add to the topic. Over time they can rewrite their first answer and improve subsequent responses.

- **The Writing Process (Developing, Fluent)**

The purpose of the writing process is to guide students through stages of creating a composition. Presented below is one version of the writing process that can be used with developing and fluent students. The version presented is a modification of the Elements of the Writing Process as described by Bos and Vaughn (1998) in their textbook.

- **Stage 1: Prewriting-** This is a preparation time, or a getting started process that allows children to think about ideas and get ready to write by focusing on a topic. Thinking of a topic to write about may be one of the most difficult tasks for students. At this point they may need assistance with brainstorming about ideas or a specific topic to write about.

  Brainstorming is the process of thinking and talking about topics the student feels confident to write about. Teachers need to encourage students to write about topics they truly enjoy. Examples include skateboarding, basketball, hockey, horseback riding, visiting an amusement park, favorite television shows, favorite things to eat, and so on. Some teachers call this the "**Brain Drain**" stage where students make a list of what they know about a topic.

- **Stage 2: Writing**- This is the composing stage where students are expected to write their first daft, or "**sloppy copy**" of their paper. The goal is to guide students to be more reflective about how they are going to address and organize the topic they have brainstormed in the first stage.

- **Stage 3: Rereading**- After a first draft is completed, students are encouraged to reread their composition to see if their writing makes sense, if something is left out (they should consult the list they dictated or wrote in the brainstorming stage), or if additional ideas should be added. This rereading is sometimes called "**Author's Mumble**", because if done properly students literally mumble to themselves as they "self-talk" to monitor the meaning of their first draft.

- **Stage 4: Revising**- Some teachers call this the "**Neat Sheet**" where students are encouraged to continue to focus on the content, or message of their paper. Students can read their draft to one or more other students, or to an adult helper in the classroom. The main questions students must keep in mind at this stage are: "Does it make sense?", "How do I connect ideas—does it flow?", and, "What else can I add to the paper that I may have left out?".

- **Stage 5: Editing**- At this stage teachers need to encourage their students to make the paper "**Goof Proof**" by having them concentrate on the mechanics of the paper such as punctuation, spelling, capitalization, and overall appearance. Some teachers prompt good editing on the part of their students by using posters or cue cards with strategies printed on them in the form of acronyms (Schumaker,

Nolan, Deshler, 1985). Figure 4.4 is an example of a COPS cue card students can use to assist them with the editing process.

Figure 4.4

A COPS Cue Card

The COPS Strategy

C   Have I **Capitalized** the first word and proper noun?
O   How is the **Overall** apearance (handwriting, margins, messy, spacing)?
P   Have I use **Punctuation** (periods, commas, semicolons)?
S   How is my **Spelling**?

- **Stage 6: Publishing**- This is the student's "**Final Fame**" in the writing process. Students can be motivated throughout the entire writing process to publish their best work. The teacher asks students to share their story orally with the class from the Author's Chair, or the piece may be displayed in the classroom or school library. Some teachers are now assisting their students with virtual publishing on the world wide internet. This is highly motivating and provides a way for student's work to reach audiences beyond the classroom, and perhaps even receive feedback via an e-mail message.

Teachers who desire more information on how to teach writing to students with disabilities should consult the following:

Bos, C. S., & Vaughn, S. (1998). *Strategies for teaching students with learning and behavior problems (4th Ed.).* Boston: Allyn and Bacon.

Kameenui, E. J., & Simmons, D. C. (1990). *Instructional strategies: The prevention of academic learning problems.* New York: Macmillan College Publishing Company, Inc.

Mason. J. M. (1989). *Reading and writing connections.* Boston: Allyn and Bacon.

Mercer, C. D., & Mercer, A. R. (1998). *Teaching students with learning problems (5th Ed.).* Upper Saddle River, New Jersey: Merrill/Prentice Hall.

Schloss, P. J., & Sedlak, R. A. (1986). *Instructional methods for students with learning and behavior problems.* Boston: Allyn and Bacon.

Part V

Analysis of a Successful Classroom
By Laurence Sargent and Suzanne Doyle

In earlier portions of this book, David Katims presented effective strategies and practices for attaining literacy by students with mental retardation. The emphasis of this chapter is to illustrate the importance of using a wide range of pedagogical strategies and techniques for facilitating learning and attaining literacy.

Teaching reading requires the balancing of strategy with direct skill based instruction (Swanson, 1999). In addition to applying these effective strategies and selecting appropriate materials, attention to classroom management practices and the affective aspects of learning appear to hold equal importance to reading methodology. We created this chapter by observing, video taping and analyzing the instruction of a highly effective teacher. Our subject serves as a special education teacher working in a Success For All (SFA) school in Colorado Springs, Colorado. In the following paragraphs we intend to paint a picture of how one highly effective teacher goes about bolstering the process of teaching reading.

- **The Context**

In the SFA model, students with special needs are taught in mainstream classes and clustered for reading instruction in non-graded functional groups. In this model, reading instruction is built on a strong structure of skill based instruction accompanied by a substantial and carefully selected body of literature. Students are assessed frequently and regrouped for reading instruction at approximately eight week intervals. Despite implementation of this highly regarded and researched instructional program, students with special needs and low language skills tend to progress slowly. At this school, the teacher in our study elected to take on the slowest and youngest group of readers in an effort to accelerate their reading growth. The students in her reading group can be characterized as having low language, poor phonemic awareness, and low readiness for reading. The group is labeled "Deep Roots" derived from the Success For All "Roots" reading program (Slavin, Madden, Wasik, Ross, Smith, & Dianda, 1996).

The general purposes of the "Deep Roots" group set forth by the teacher were to:
- Build on language familiar to the students
- Increase writing and use of graphics
- Increase phonemic awareness
- Pace instruction to allow for repetition and skill mastery.

All of the students in the "Deep Roots" group represented at-risk factors including mild mental retardation, learning disabilities, traumatic brain injury, English as a second language, and at-risk life experiences represented by high mobility and low income.

Section I: Watching the Lesson Unfold

- **Entry**

At the designated time, twelve cheerful children entered the classroom one by one. Upon entry, the teacher made eye contact with each child and exchanged warm words of greeting or acknowledgement. Observers concluded that students were instantly given the impression that they were valued. It was obvious to the observers that much work had proceeded establishing a positive classroom climate. Students quickly arranged themselves in a semi-circle at a location within the classroom set up for this purpose. This movement occurred with minimal verbal instruction and a gesture or two. Recorded classical music played in the background giving the classroom a calm and relaxed feeling.

- **Antecedent Set**

The lesson began with a step familiar to all who are trained in direct instruction procedures. Through questioning, the teacher reviewed the previous story using free input from students and followed it with a structured review. The structured review involved providing students with stem statements and having them complete them from their memory of the story from the previous day. Each stem was presented in the sequence provided in the story. During the exchange between the teacher and students, social skills such as raising hands before speaking and waiting turns were cued and modeled by the teacher.

- **Presenting the Elements of Reading**

After review of the previous day's work, the teacher began preparing students to read a new story. Many of the steps observed resembled procedures recommended in the work of Mari Clay (1993) for emergent readers. These steps include:
  - Posting the title in front of the group
  - Introducing the names of the author and illustrator
  - Introduction of the names of the characters in the story about to be read
  - Introducing and rehearsing new vocabulary.

In addition, the teacher did the following:
  - Posed problem in the story to the students.
  - Discussed possible solutions to the problem.
  - Prepared and introduced students to food reinforcers associated with the content of the story.

Throughout the presentation and discussion with the students, our teacher modeled, cued, and reinforced appropriate social skills in the form of saying please and thank you, taking turns, waiting for others to finish talking, and using silent gestures to obtain teacher attention.

- **Reading to the Students**

As the story Little Red Ridinghood was read to the students, the teacher acted out the roles of each of the characters. She carefully acted the parts with a degree of reserve that sustained attention but prevented student from becoming overly excited. During the course of reading the story, the teacher used gentle touch and proximity control to maintain attention of students who struggled to stay focused on the story. As the story was read and discussion ensued, the teacher maintained intense eye contact with each child as he or she spoke. She also politely redirected off topic comments typical of this age group.

After the reading, a discussion followed where new vocabulary was emphasized and the problem and solutions posed in the story were discussed. In the question and answer phase of the discussion, students received frequent verbal praise for correct responses. When asking questions, the teacher used a visible three finger silent count before calling on students to answer. The teacher used gestures to prompt and cue students' responses on letter sounds. The students all used hand gestures to indicate when they knew the answer to a question. The teacher modeled correct responding. The use of gestures appeared to reduce the potential for "blurting out" behavior observed in many other classrooms. To illustrate and reinforce success, the teacher had students place plastic golf balls in a clear plastic cylinder. Filling the cylinder represented attainment of a lesson objective for that day, and in a way, it represented a three dimensional bar graph.

During the questioning portion of the lessons, the teacher never told students directly when their responses were wrong. Each was told they made a good try, but suggested he or she could fix their answer a bit to make it better. Self-correction efforts were lauded and students comfortably risked making errors as they attempted to repair their answers. When students struggled to make corrections, other students were asked to help the struggling student.

The notion of helping each other was strongly reinforced and emphasized throughout the lesson.

- **Reading Activity**

  After the reading of the story, the teacher led the whole group through a choral reading exercise. Questions on the content of the reading followed. The new and unfamiliar language was reintroduced and discussed. Language unfamiliar to the students was covered extensively. For example, the students had no understanding of the phrase "tripped down the path." The closest they could come without explanation had to do with falling. During the discussion, the teacher continued to imbed social skills instruction into the lesson. For example she cued the students by saying "Look at me. I am going to give you a compliment." After modeling the compliment, she asked the students to give each reader compliments.

- **Cooperative Learning**

  Following the choral reading and discussion, students broke up into two person teams and were sent to various parts of the room to engage in paired reading. All students initiated the reading task promptly, but a few needed prompting to remain on task during the paired reading portion of the lesson. The teacher set a timer to indicate when this part of the class period would end. When the timer buzzed, all students proceeded to the circle area to receive new instructions.

- **The Writing Task**

  After settling into their spots in the semi-circle, the teacher handed out the following from pre-positioned materials: floor tiles to use as hard surface lap boards, paper, and pencils. She began this portion of the daily lesson by modeling completion of the writing task. In addition, she presented previous examples of the students' writing and writing and carefully pointed out where they had completed the whole task. The teacher and students applauded the examples presented. Somehow without feeling that it was out of context, the teacher embedded another social skills topic regarding "how to talk about a playground game without boasting."

After modeling and presenting students work, the teacher established explicit criteria for students on their writing task. Each student was to write no less than three sentences and to be certain that the sentences had proper punctuation. Before putting the students to work, the teacher set a clear standard for how students were to transition to tables or other areas of the room for the writing activity. Students were sent to new locations in pairs, thus avoiding rushing and bumping that can result in behavioral conflicts.

Section II: The Analysis

The observers found that the content and methods used specifically to teach reading were standard for the Success For All model of instruction. The virtues of the lesson were represented in the many effective pedagogical processes employed to assure that students learned. The following paragraphs present the analysis of instruction observed.

• Creation of the Learning Climate

Clearly, this teacher put considerable thought and effort into establishing a positive classroom climate for learning. Through intense eye contact and personal communication, each student received individual attention that conveyed a message that the teacher valued him or her. Polite and warm treatment of one another was modeled and reinforced. Further, the teacher used correction procedures that assured students would perform accurately and not feel degraded in the process.

In addition to the teacher making each student feel valued, she arranged and prompted opportunities for students to say things to other students that were reaffirming. Thus, the climate created represented two of the most important components of a well functioning classroom: students felt valued by their teacher and by their classmates.

- ## Classroom Management and Discipline

The rituals and rules of the classroom had been taught early on in the semester. Students responded to the various signals when it was time to change the activity. In discussion with the teacher, she reported that she spent the first week of instruction on how to follow the class rituals before seriously attempting to teach reading. Other characteristics of classroom management were evident by the careful preparation and placement of materials. When the teacher was ready to teach a new part of the lesson, materials for the upcoming activity were close at hand.

Planning and allowances were also made for students who had difficulty sitting and staying on task. High activity students were frequently given intermittent duties that would get them on their feet and moving. Some examples were:
- "Get me that book."
- "Bring me my timer."
- "Put the balls in the tube."
- "Pass out these papers."
- "Pass out the little muffins."

During the course of the lesson, the teacher used non-verbal as well as verbal redirects to maintain attention to task. There was never a necessity during our observations to use stern or harsh word to attain student compliance.

- ## Teaching Social Skills

Perhaps due to her several years of experience, the teacher adeptly took advantage of opportunities related to the topic or student comments during discussion to directly teach and reinforce a variety of social skills. She modeled and reinforced polite and cooperative behavior frequently. The students also received praise when they modeled appropriate social behavior.

- **Time On-task and Multiple Activities**

  Due to the age and backgrounds of the students, the teacher prepared well for dealing with short attention spans. Most of the activities lasted less than ten minutes and movement was incorporated into each of the transitions between activities. Although some settling had to occur at the beginning of each activity, students were observed engaging in the activities without becoming distracted. Some students had difficulty initiating activity for independent tasks such as writing, but the teacher prompted them through the steps as she moved from student to student.

- **Classroom Arrangement and Environment**

  The teacher arranged the classroom in a way that established a different function for each part of the classroom. The sections of the room were set up to allow students to move from the semi-circle, to the writing area with tables and chairs and then to the centers area in roughly a clockwise rotation.

  The room was decorated with materials that reinforced the curriculum. Letters in different forms were posted at the front of the circle area. Vowels were posted on the walls and language cards were posted in three different wall hung pocket charts.

- **Self-Efficacy**

  Perhaps most important, the students believed themselves to be readers. Due to the positive climate of the classroom and high rates of time on task, students demonstrated a willingness to take risks and persist at tasks that given their disabilities or background would be difficult.

Summary

The earlier portions of this book present effective strategies and practices for teaching reading to students with mental retardation and developmental disabilities. In addition to applying research based practices for teaching reading, highly effective teachers attend to:

- Creating a positive classroom environment where children feel valued by their teacher and peers.
- Planning for management of the classroom by pre-positioning materials, practicing classroom rituals and signals, and providing opportunities for movement.
- Embedding social skills training into all aspects of instruction.
- Assuring on-task behavior by adjusting and alternating activities to include novelty and movement.
- Providing wait time for students to process questions and make responses.
- Arranging the classroom to prevent students from interfering with one another, as well as, creating a n environment that supports the curriculum.
- Supporting and reinforcing development of the sense of self-efficacy in the students. (Students who believe that can read will persist longer at learning to read better.)

The teacher engaged in many practices recommended by Katims earlier in this book. Some of those included reading familiar and predictable literature, cueing students to brainstorm and make predictions, and teaching use of semantic and syntatical cues. She also presented and reinforced decoding strategies in the context of reading literature. In addition, the teacher had the students engage in writing on the topics covered in the reading lesson.

The observers concluded that this group of at risk learners were on their way to achieving literacy. In addition to the elements of effective reading instructions, attention to the affective components of teaching created happy, risk taking and persistent learners.

Reference List

Adams, M. J. (1990). *Beginning to read: Thinking and learning about print.* Cambridge, MA: The MIT press.

Butler, D. (1975). Cushla and her books. NY: Penguin Books.

Cawley, J. F., & Parmar, R. S. (1995). Comparisons of reading and reading-related tasks among students with average intellectual ability and students with mild mental retardation. *Education and Training in Mental Retardation and Developmental Disabilities,* 30, 118-129.

Cegelka, P. A., & Cegelka, W. J. (1970). A review of research: Reading and the educable mentally handicapped. *Exceptional Children,* 37, 187-200.

Clay, M. (1993). *Reading Recovery.* London: Heinemann Educational Books.

Clay, M. (1975). *What did I write?* London: Heinemann Educational Books.

Conners, F. A. (1992). Reading instruction for students with moderate mental retardation: Review and analysis of research. American Journal of Mental Retardation, 96, 577-597.

Cunningham, P. M., & Cunningham, D. P. (1992). Making Words: Enhancing the invented spelling-decoding connection. *The Reading Teacher,* 46, 106-116.

Dunn, L. M. (1956). A comparison of the reading processes of mentally retarded boys of the same mental age. In L. M. Dunn & R. J. Capobianco (Eds.), Studies of reading and arithmetic in mentally retarded boys. *Monograph of the society for research and child development,* 19, 7-99.

Hedrick, W. B., Katims, D. S., & Carr, N. J. (1999). Implementing a multi-method multi-level literacy program for students with mild to moderate mental retardation.

Katims, D. S. (2000). Literacy instruction for people with mental retardation: Historical highlights and contemporary analysis. *Education and training in mental retardation and developmental disabilities*, 35,3-15.

Katims, D. S. (1999). Literacy Assessment of Students With Mental Retardation: Analysis and Description. Manuscript submitted for publication.

Katims, D. S. (1996). The emergence of literacy in elementary students with mild retardation. *Focus on Autism and Other Developmental Disabilities*, 11, 147-157.

Katims, D. S. (1994). Emergence of literacy in preschool children with disabilities. *Learning Disability Quarterly*, 17, 58-71.

Katims, D. S. (1991). Emergent literacy in early childhood special education: Curriculum and instruction. *Topics in Early Childhood Special Education*, 11, 69-84.

Katims, D. S., & Pierce, P. L. (1995). Literacy-rich environments and the transition of young children with special needs. *Topics in Early Childhood Special Education*, 15, 219-234.

Martinez, M., & Teale, W. H. (1988). Reading in a kindergarten classroom library. *The Reading Teacher*, 41, 568-572.

Morrow, L. M. (1993). *Literacy development in the early years: Helping children read and write (2nd Ed.)*. Boston: Allyn and Bacon.

Ogle, D. M. (1986). K-W-L: A teaching model that develops active reading of expository text. *The Reading Teacher,* 39, 564-570.

Orlando, C. P. (1973). Review of the reading research in special education. In L. Mann & D. A. Sabatino (Eds.), *The first review of special education*. Philadelphia: JSE Press.

Schloss, P. J., Harriman, N., & Pfiefer, K. (1985). Application of a sequential prompt reduction technique to the independent composition performance of behaviorally disordered youth. *Behavioral Disorders*, 11, 17-23.

Schumaker, J. B., Nolan, S. M., & Deshler, D. D. (1985). *The error monitoring strategy.* Lawrence: KS: The University of Kansas.

Singh, N. N., & Singh, J. (1986). Reading acquisition and remediation in the mentally retarded. In N. R. Ellis & N. W. Bray (Eds.), *International review of research in mental retardation* (Vol. 14, pp. 165-199). New York: Academic Press, Inc.

Slavin, R.E., Madden, N.A., Dolan, L.J., Wasik, B.A., Ross, S., Smith, L. & Dianda, M. (1996). Success for All: A summary of research. *Journal of Education for Students Placed at Risk*, 1(1), 41-76.

Stanovich, K. E. (1985). Cognitive determinants of reading in mentally retarded individuals. In N. R. Ellis (Ed.), *International review of research in mental retardation* (Vol. 13, pp. 181-214). New York: Academic Press.

Sulzby, E. (1989). Forms of writing and rereading from writing. In J. Mason (Ed.), *Reading and writing connections.* Needham Heights, MA: Allyn & Bacon.

Swanson, H. L. (1999). Reading research for students with LD: A meta-analysis of intervention outcomes. *Journal of Learning Disabilities*, 32, 504-529.

Tompkins, G. E., & Webeler, M. (1983). What will happen next? Using predictable books with young children. *The Reading Teacher*, 36, 498-502.

United States Department of Education (1996). *Learning to read, reading to learn.* Office of Special Education Programs. Washington, DC: Author.

Recommended Predictable Books for Students

Brown, M. (1961). *The Three Billy Goats Gruff.* William R. Scott.

Brown, M. (1947). *Goodnight Moon.* Harper & Row.

Carle, E. (1977). *The Grouchy Ladybug.* Crowell.

Carle, E. (1969). *The Very Hungry Caterpillar.* Collins World.

Flack, M. (1952). *Ask Mr. Bear.* Macmillan.

Galdone, P. (1975). *The Gingerbread Boy.* Houghton Mifflin.

Galdone, P. (1973). *The Little Red Hen.* Scholastic Press.

Galdone, P. (1973). *The Three Billy Goats Gruff.* Seabury Press.

Galdone, P. (1972). *The Three Bears.* Scholastic Press.

Galdone, P. (1970). *The Three Little Pigs.* Seabury Press.

Galdone, P. (1968). *Henny Penny.* Scholastic Press.

Hutchins, P. (1972). *Good-Night, Owl!* Macmillan.

Hutchins, P. (1971). *Titch.* Collier Books.

Martin, B, Jr. (1983). *Brown Bear, Brown Bear, What Do You See?* Holt, Rinehart and Winston.

Rosen, M. (1989). *We're Going on a Bear Hunt.* Macmillan.

Sendak, M. (1964). *Where the Wild Things Are.* Harper & Row.

Sendak, M. (1962). *Chicken Soup With Rice.* Scholastic Press.

Williams, S. (1990). *I Went Walking.* Harcourt.

Wood, A. (1984). *The Napping House.* Harcourt.